FOR ORGANS, PIANOS & ELECTRONIC KEYBOARDS

E-Z PLAY TODAY

43

SING ALONG REQUESTS

D1305827

E-Z does it! That's why E-Z Play TODAY Music was created. This series has been designed with a special music notation for instant playing enjoyment.

The collection of songs in each book has been specifically arranged for use with all major brand organs, including chord organs and those with automatic chord units. Special chord notation is also included for the triad and conventional chord player. The entire series provides a play-on-sight repertoire filled with musical fun for everyone . . . delightful tunes that will appeal to every musical interest.

Before you begin your "E-Z" adventure, read the next two pages for a "playing preview" of the special notation and a full explanation of the chord symbols used throughout the series. If this is your first encounter with organ music, you'll be able to enjoy instant playing fun. If you've had previous organ playing experience, you'll enjoy having a complete variety of music at your fingertips. In any case, there are hours of musical fun ahead for everyone.

Contents

HAL•LEONARD
CORPORATION

7777 W. BLUEMOUND RD. P.O. BOX 13819 MILWAUKEE, WI 53213

Playing Preview

THE MELODY (Right Hand)

The melody of a song appears as large lettered notes on a staff. The letter name corresponds to a key on the keyboard of an organ.

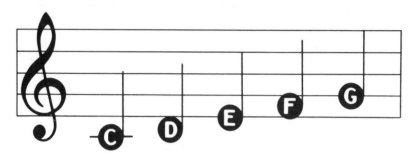

ACCOMPANIMENT (Left Hand)

The arrangements in this series have been written for all types of chord accompaniment.

1 One button (chord organ) or one-key chords.

2 Three-note (triad) chords.

3 Conventional, or standard chord positions.

Chord names, called chord symbols, appear above the melody line as either a boxed symbol $\boxed{\text{C}}$

or as an alternate chord (**C7**)

or both $\overset{\textbf{C7}}{\boxed{\text{C}}}$

1 For chord organ or one-key chords, play whichever chord name is on your unit.

2 If you are playing triad chords, follow the boxed symbols. A triad chord is played like this:

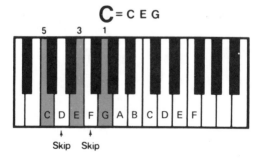

● Place your little finger on the key which has the same letter name as the chord.

● Skip a white key and place your middle finger on the next white key.

● Skip another white key and place your thumb on the next white key.

In some cases, there is an ARROW to the **left** or to the **right** of the chord name.

The arrow indicates moving one of the triad notes either to the **left** or to the **right** on the keyboard.

To understand this, first think of a chord symbol as having three sections, representing the three notes of the chord.

An ARROW is positioned next to the chord letter in one of these sections, indicating which of the three notes to change. For example:

• An arrow to the left means to move a note of the chord **down** (left) to the next adjacent key.

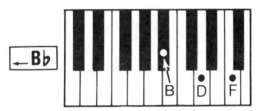

In this example where the arrow is in the **lower left**, or "1" position, move the first note "B" **down** to the black key B♭.

• An arrow to the right means to move a note of the chord **up** (right) to the next adjacent key.

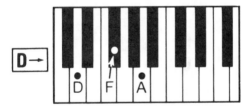

In this example where the arrow is in the **middle**, or "2" position, move the middle note **up** to the black key F♯.

3 If you are playing standard chord positions, play the chord in the boxed symbol, unless an alternate chord is indicated. Play alternate chords whenever possible.

For your reference, a Chord Speller Chart of standard chord positions appears in the back of this book.

REGISTRATION AND RHYTHM

A Registration number is shown above the music for each song. This number corresponds to the same number on the Registration Guide which appears on the inside front cover of this book. The Registration numbers also correspond to the numbers on the E-Z Play TODAY Registration Guides that are available for many brands of organs. See your organ dealer for the details.

You may wish to select your own favorite registration or perhaps experiment with different voice combinations. Then add an automatic rhythm...and HAVE FUN.

Ain't She Sweet

Words by Jack Yellen
Music by Milton Ager

Registration 3

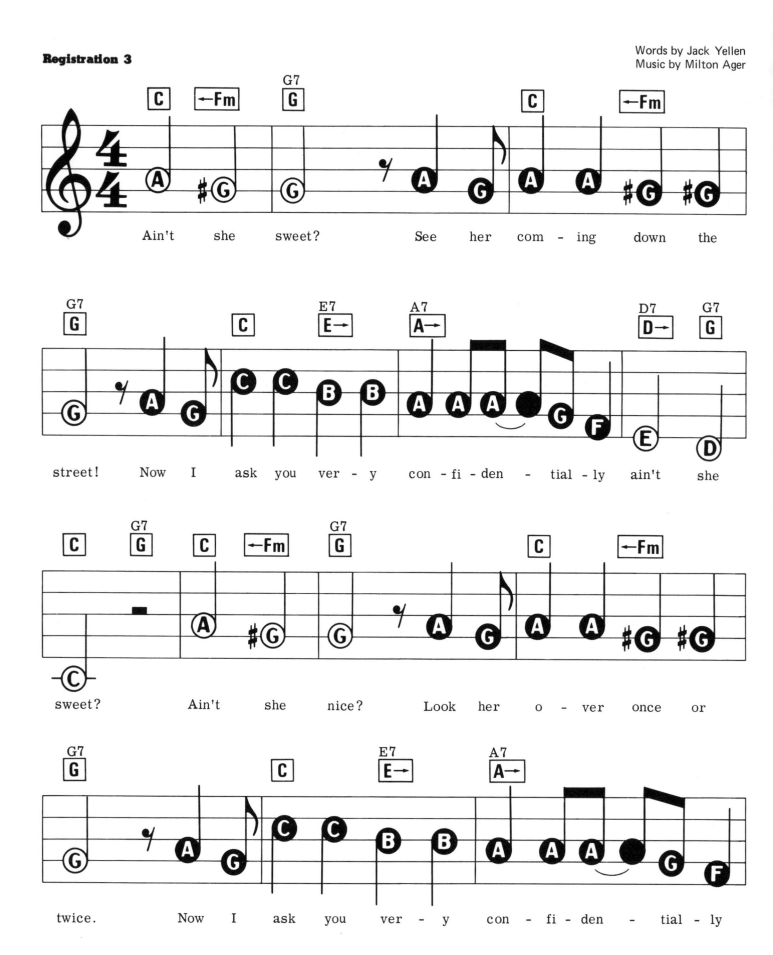

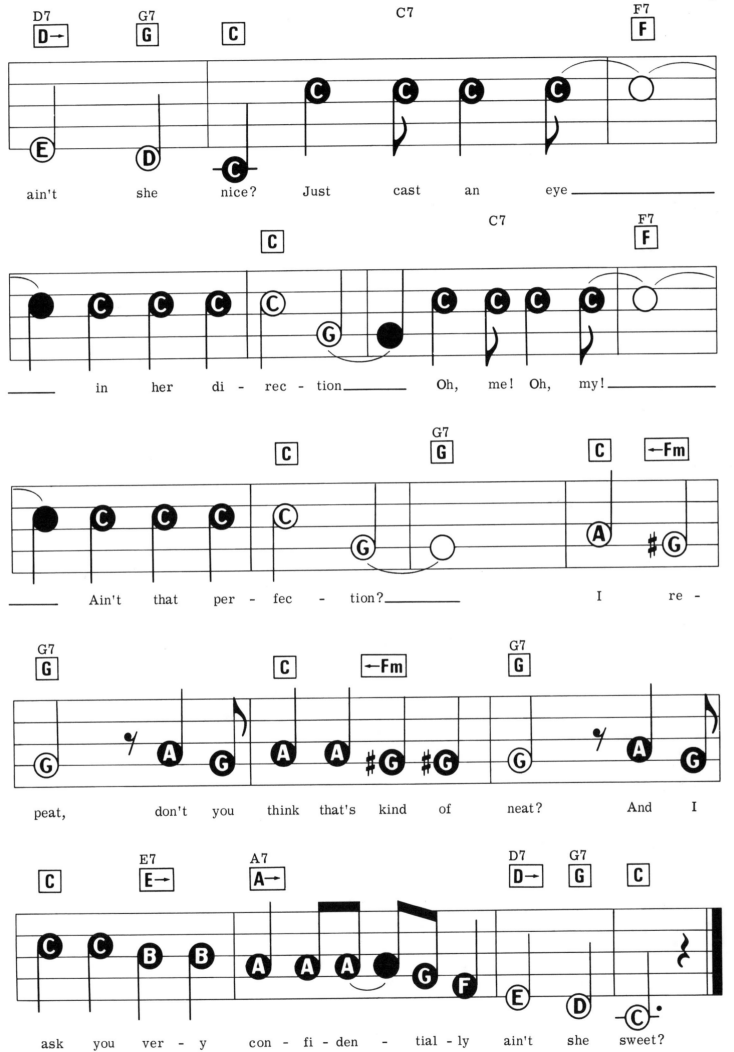

Ain't We Got Fun

Words by Gus Kahn and Raymond B. Egan
Music by Richard A. Whiting

Registration 5

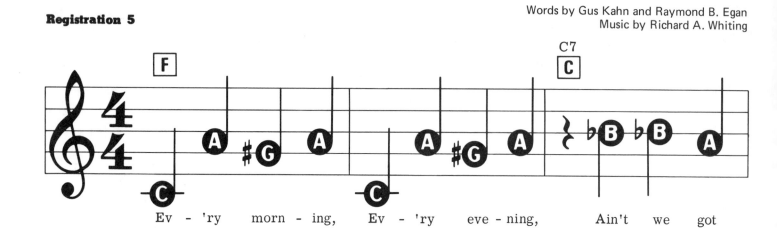

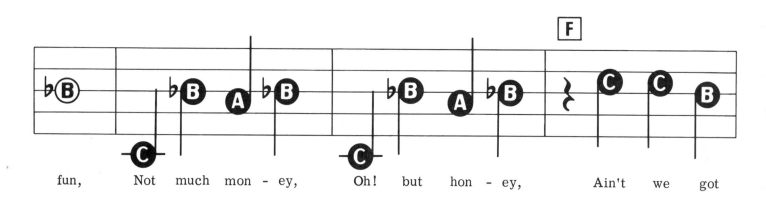

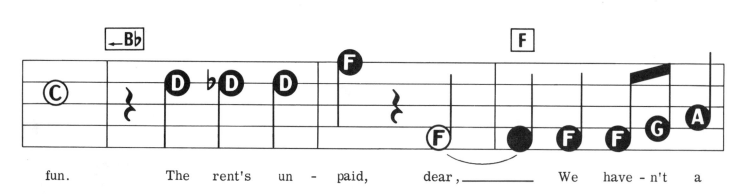

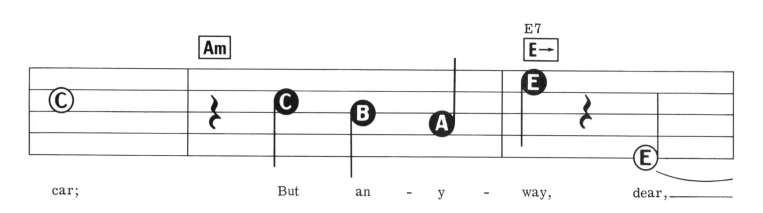

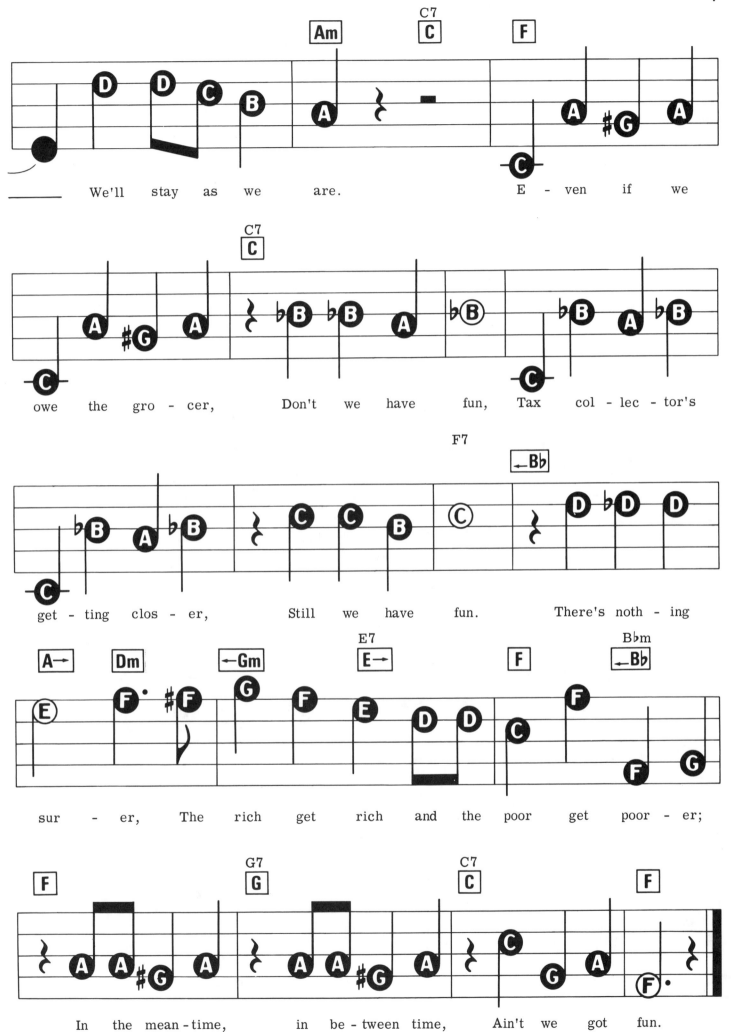

Baby Face

Words and Music by Benny Davis
and Harry Akst

Registration 9

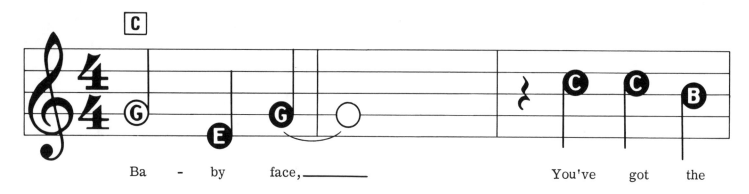

Ba - by face, _____ You've got the

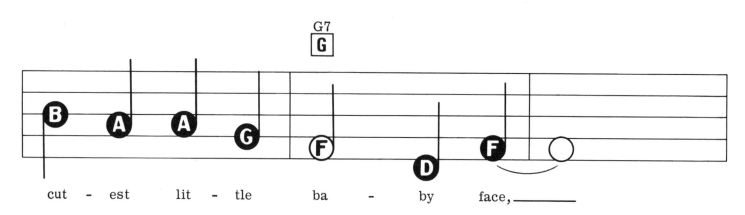

cut - est lit - tle ba - by face, _____

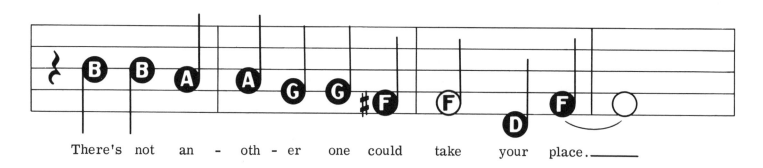

There's not an - oth - er one could take your place. _____

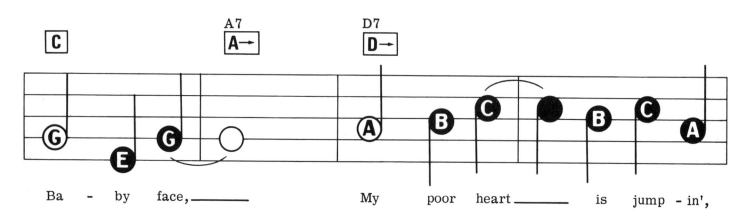

Ba - by face, _____ My poor heart _____ is jump - in',

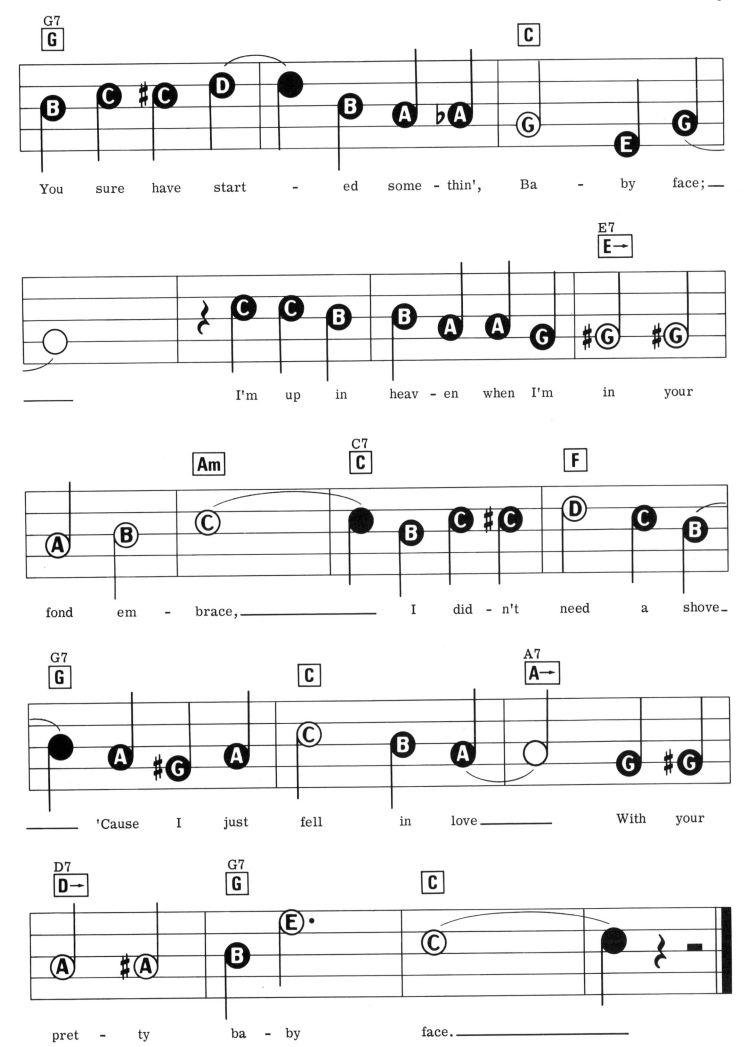

Bye Bye Blackbird

Words by Mort Dixon
Music by Ray Henderson

Registration 2

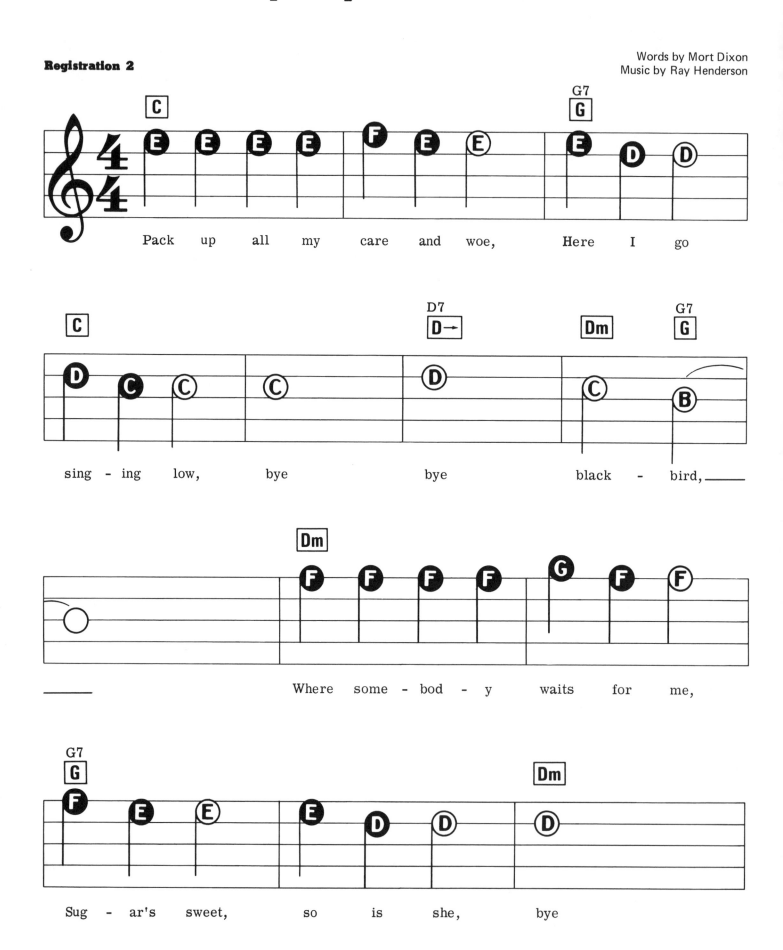

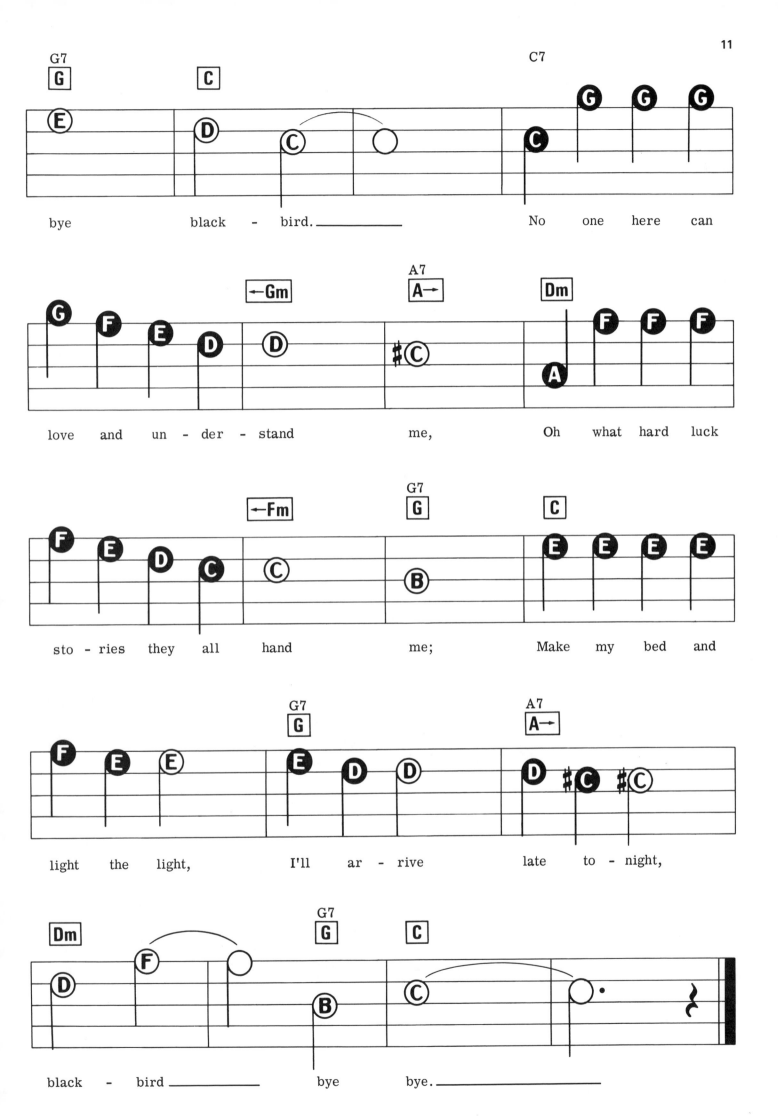

California Here I Come

Words and Music by Al Jolson,
Bud DeSylva and Joseph Meyer

Registration 5

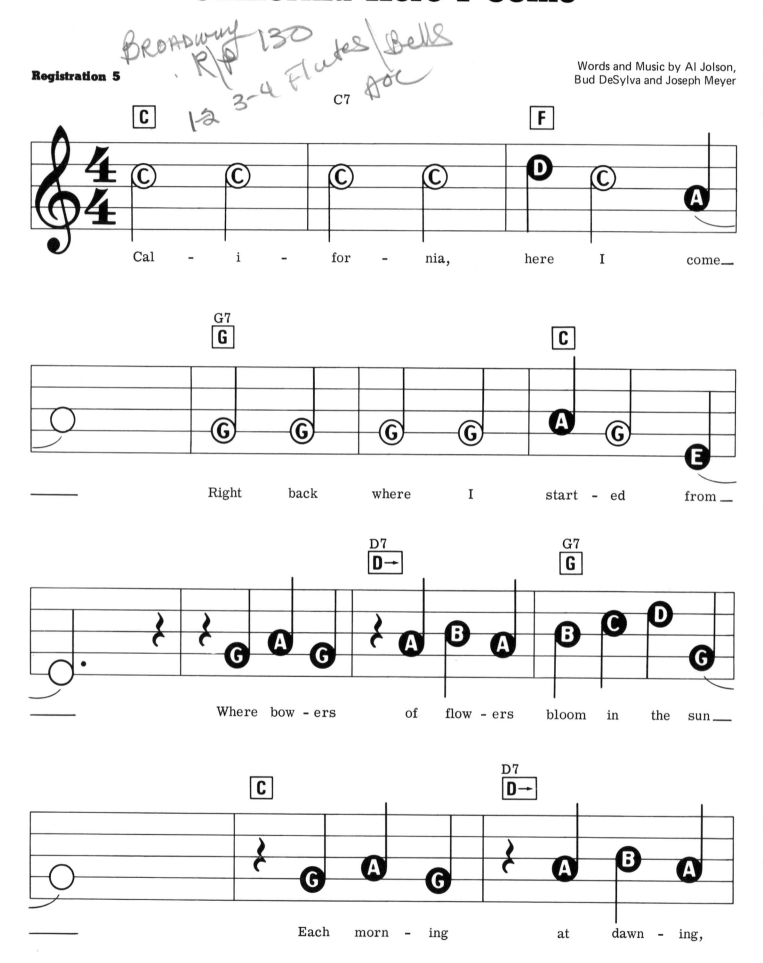

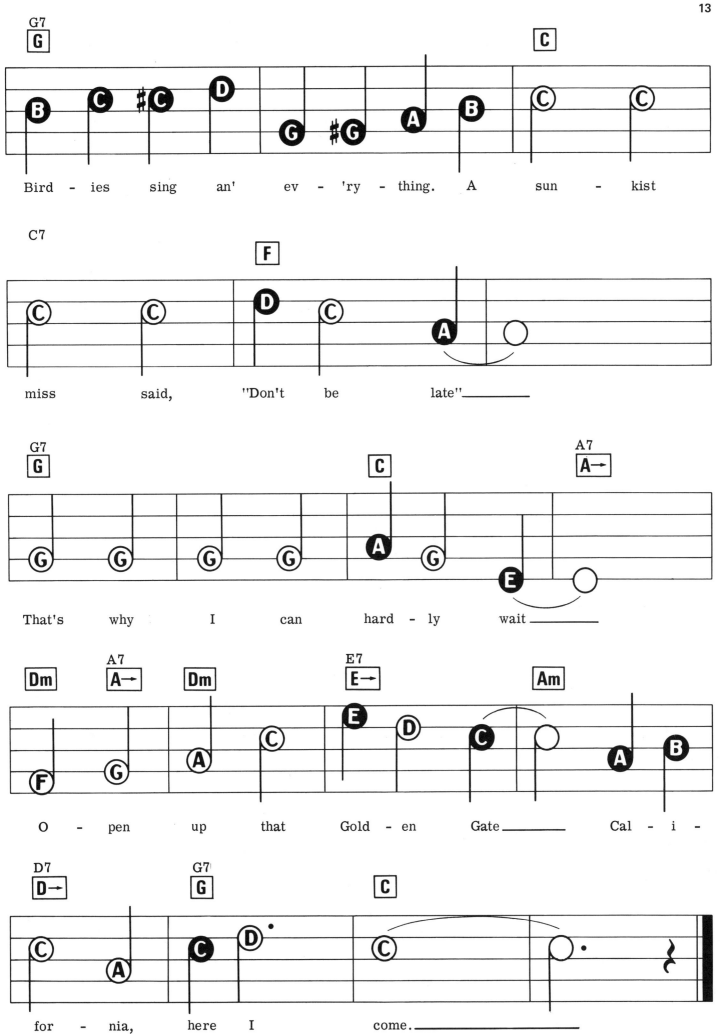

Chinatown, My Chinatown

Words by William Jerome
Music by Jean Schwartz

Registration 4

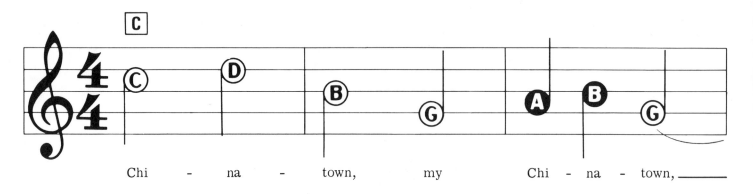

Chi - na - town, my Chi - na - town, _____

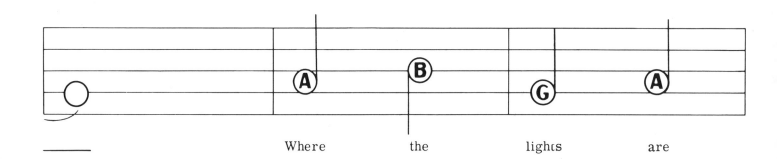

_____ Where the lights are

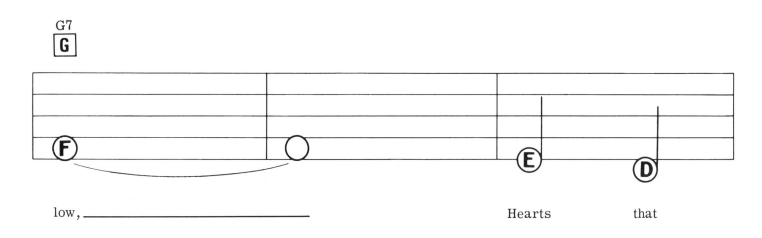

low, _____ Hearts that

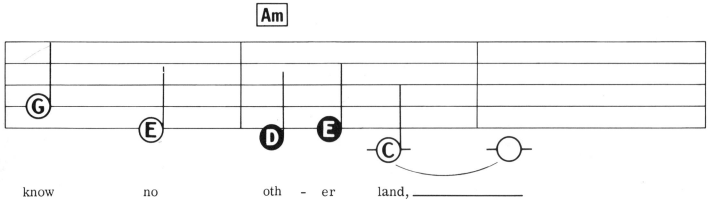

know no oth - er land, _____

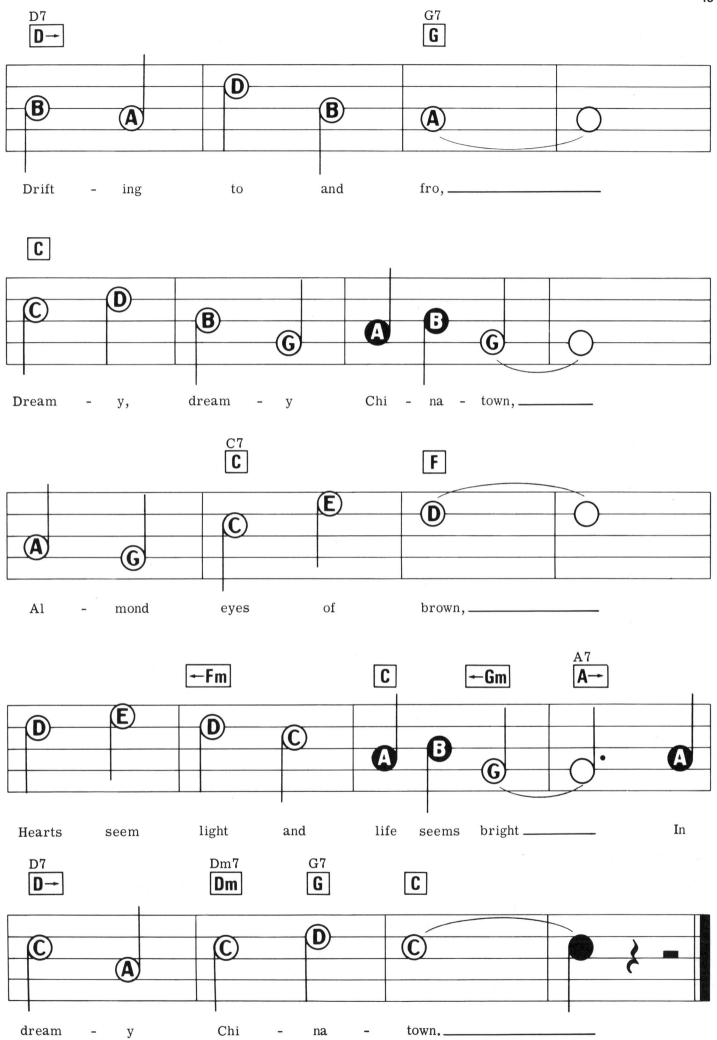

Cuddle Up A Little Closer, Lovey Mine

Registration 3

Words by Otto Harbach
Music by Karl Hoschna

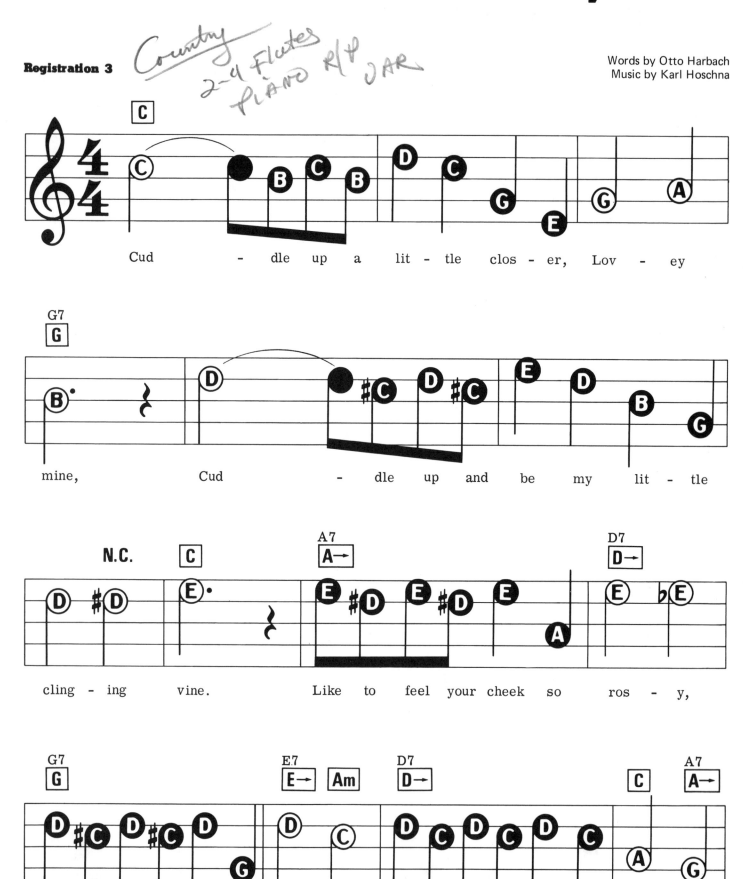

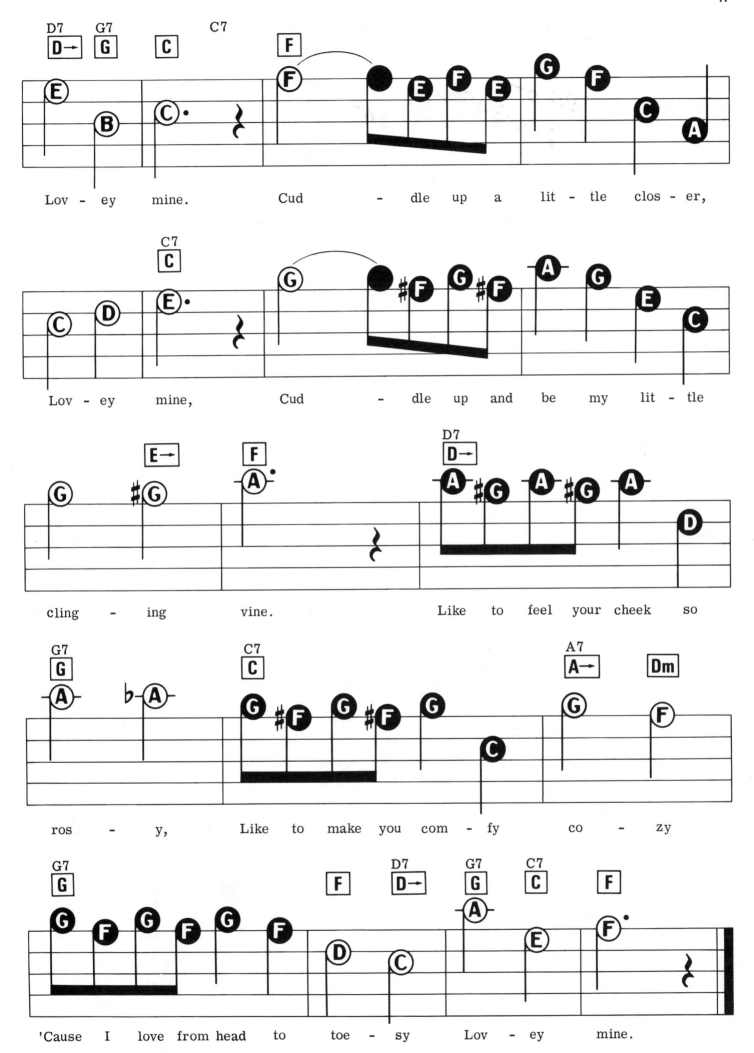

Happy Days Are Here Again

Words by Jack Yellen
Music by Milton Ager

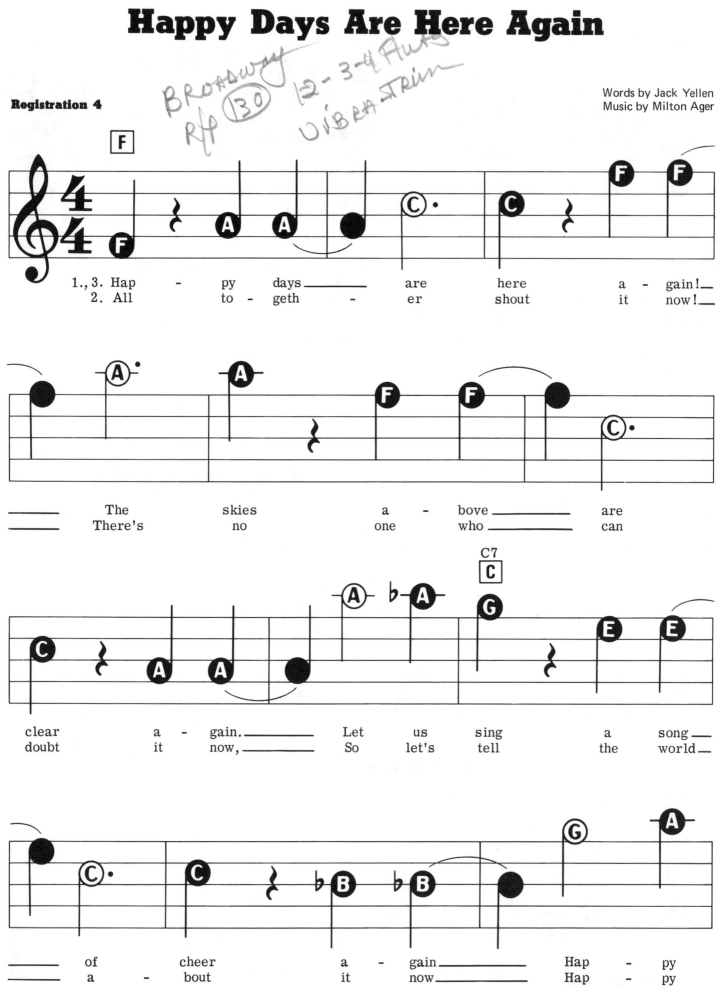

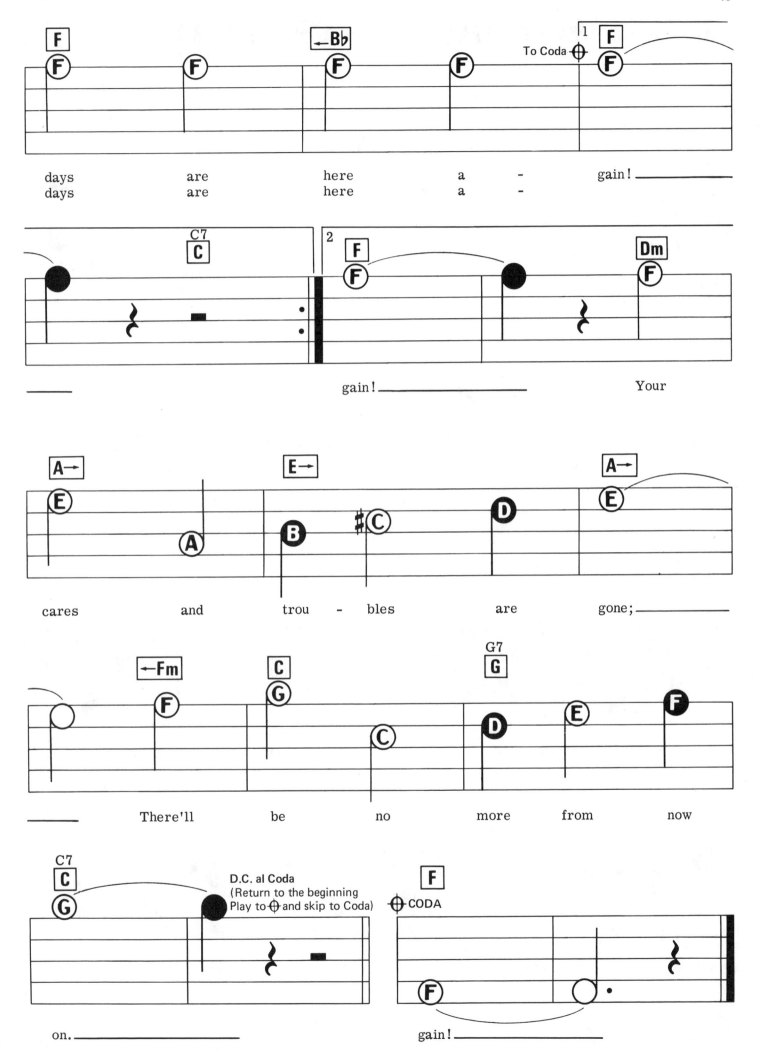

If You Were The Only Girl In The World

Words by Clifford Grey
Music by Nat D. Ayer

Registration 10

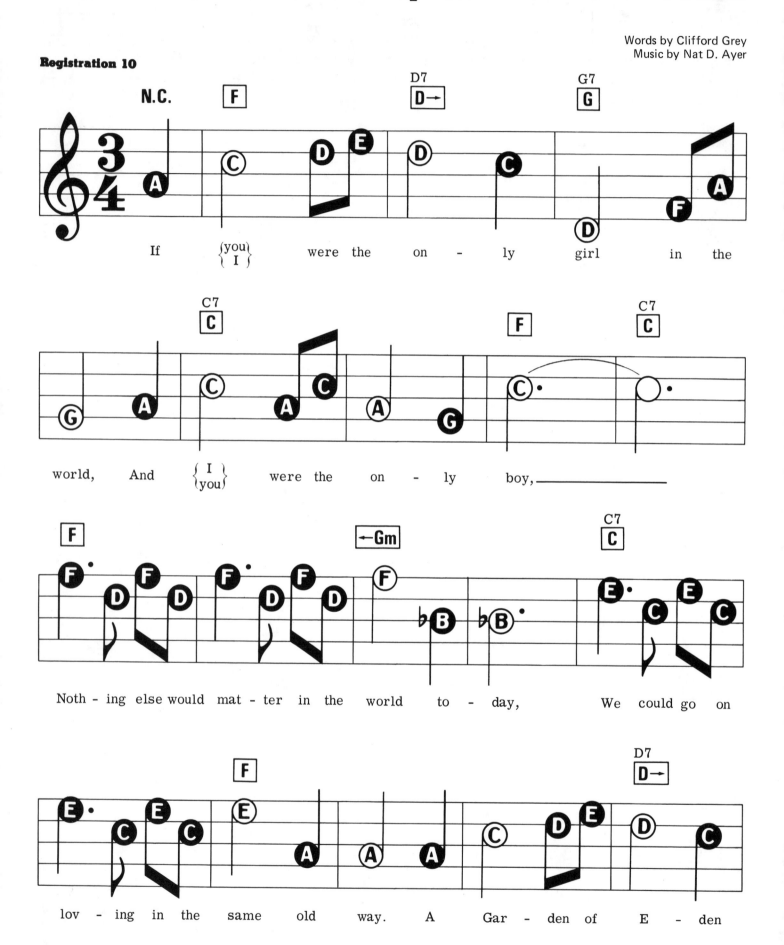

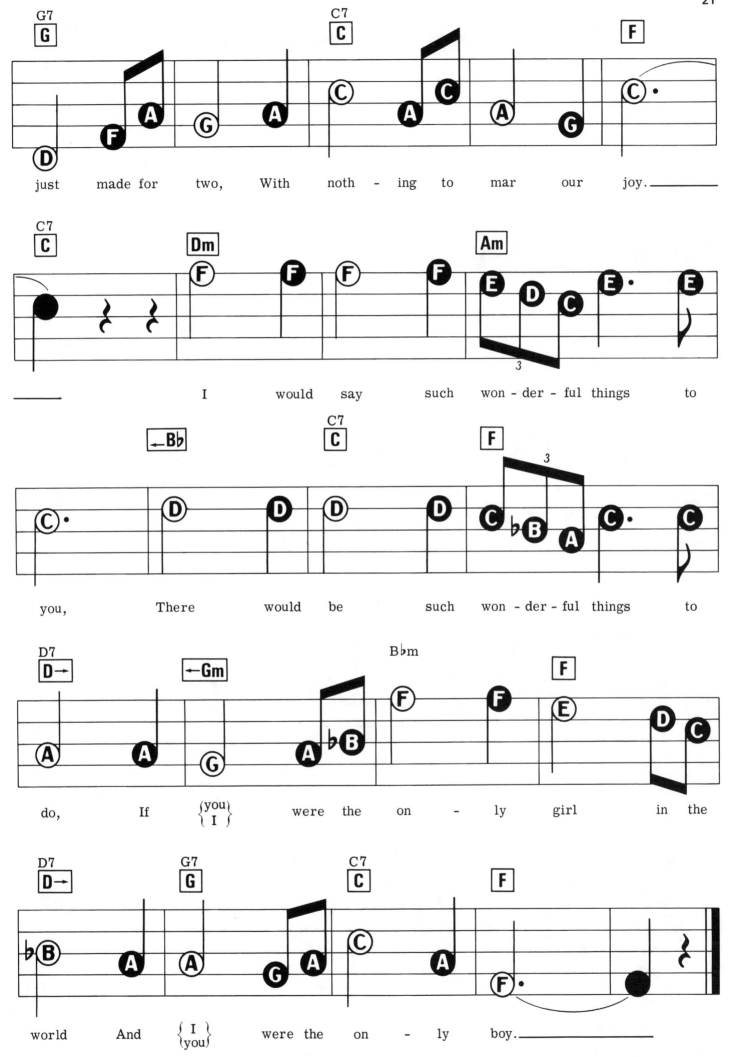

I'm Forever Blowing Bubbles

Words and Music by Jaan Kenbrovin
and John William Kellette

Registration 5

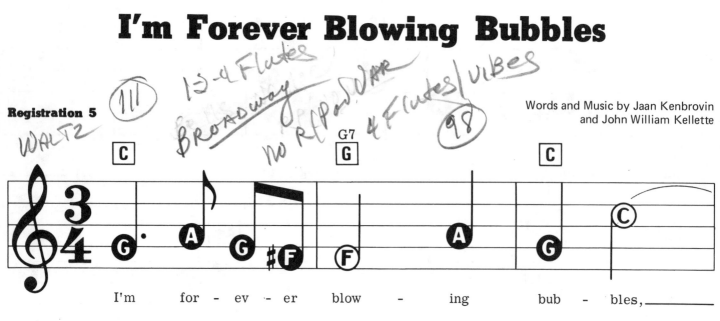

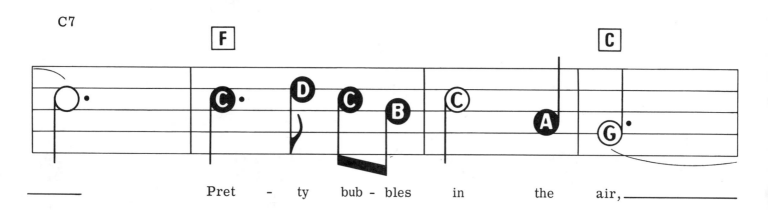

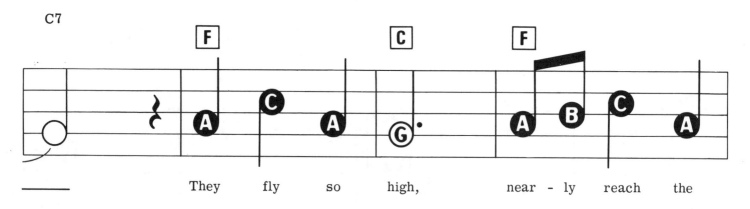

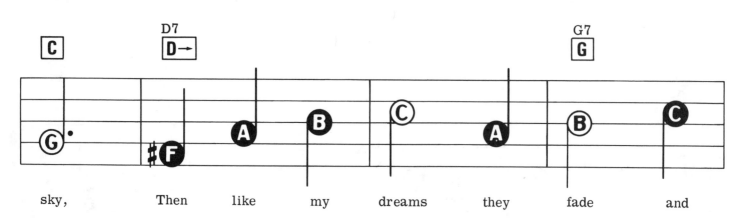

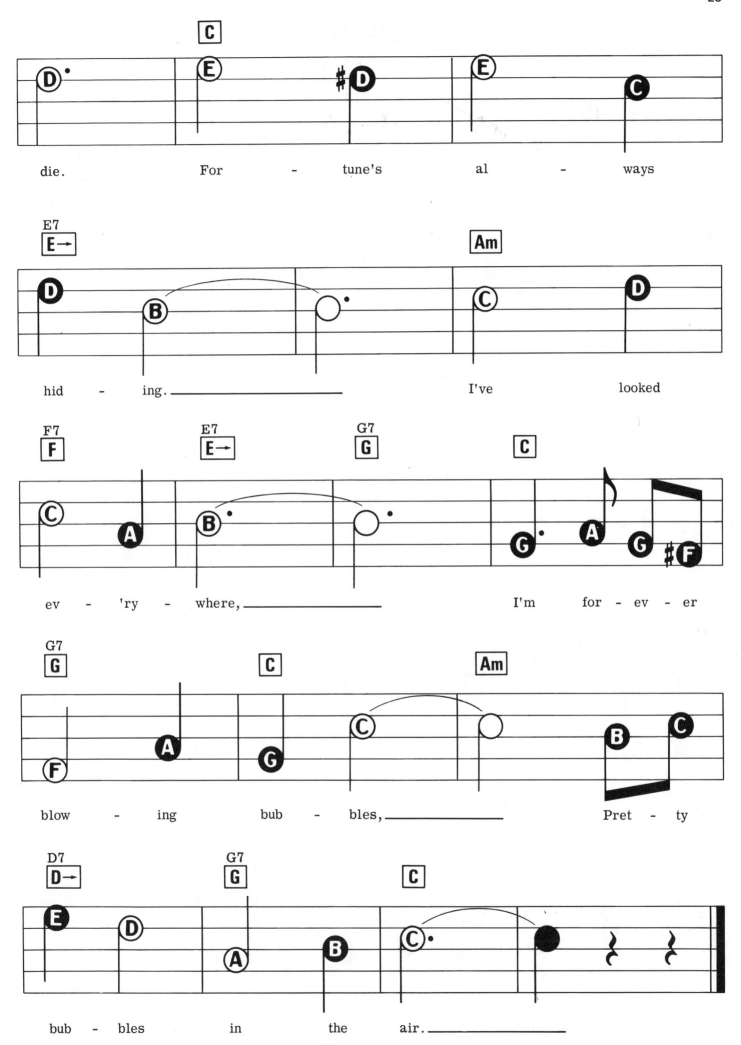

I'm Just Wild About Harry

Words and Music by Noble Sissle
and Eubie Blake

Registration 3

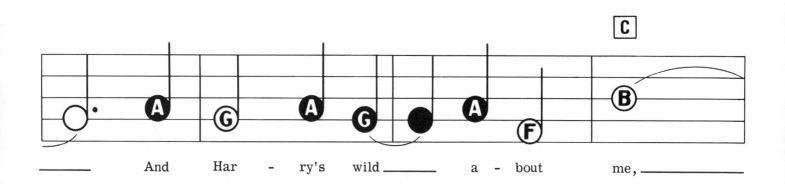

I'm just wild _____ a - bout Har - ry, _____

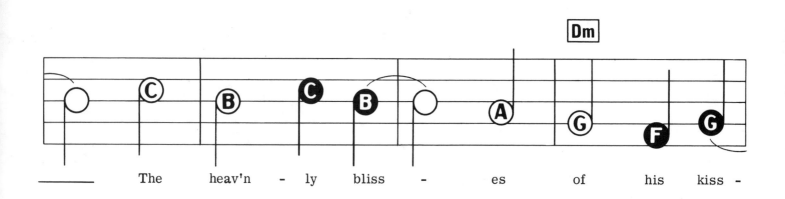

_____ And Har - ry's wild _____ a - bout me, _____

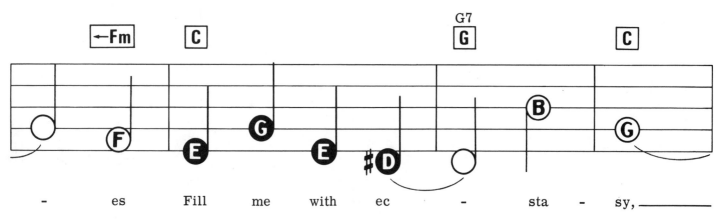

_____ The heav'n - ly bliss - es of his kiss -

- es Fill me with ec - sta - sy, _____

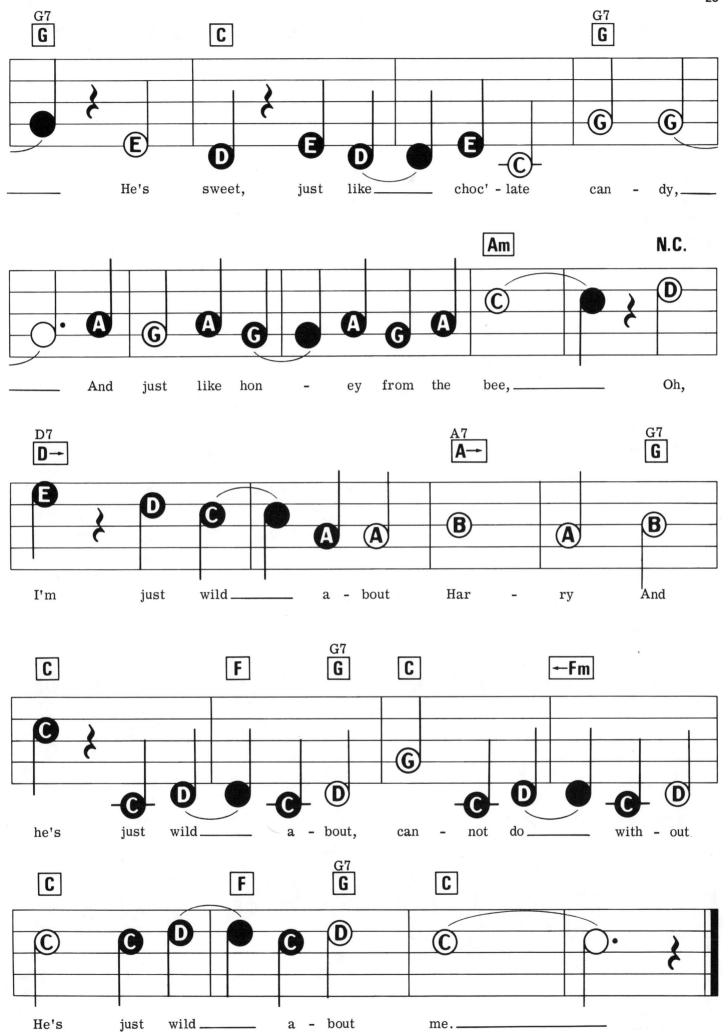

I'm Looking Over A Four Leaf Clover

Registration 4

Words by Mort Dixon
Music by Harry Woods

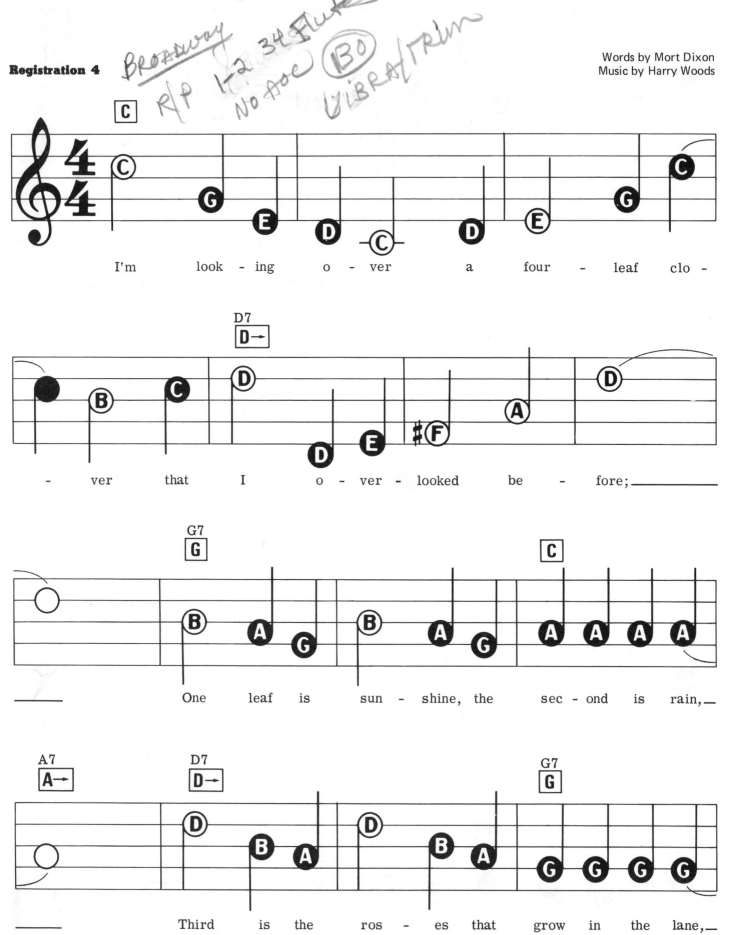

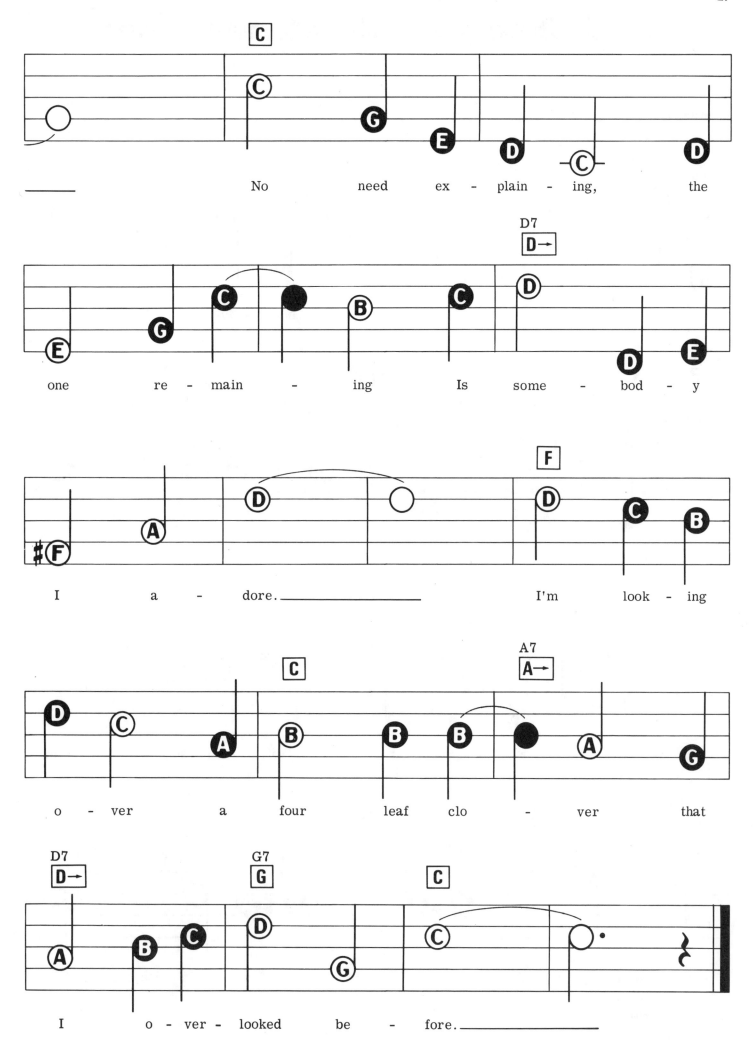

In A Shanty In Old Shanty Town

Words by John Siras and Joe Young
Music by Little Jack Little

Registration 2

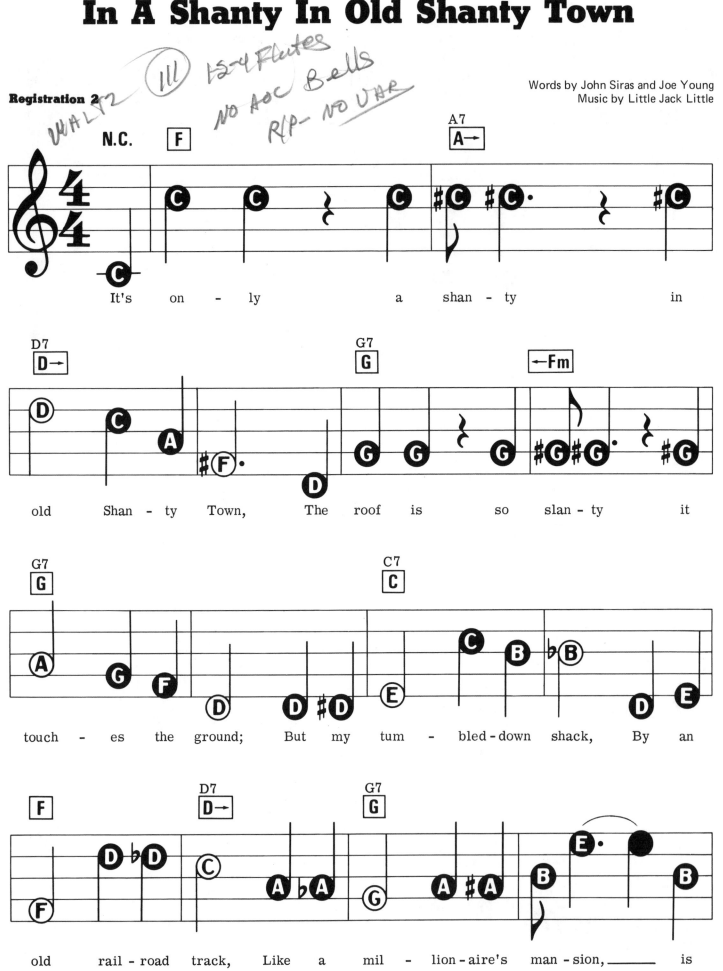

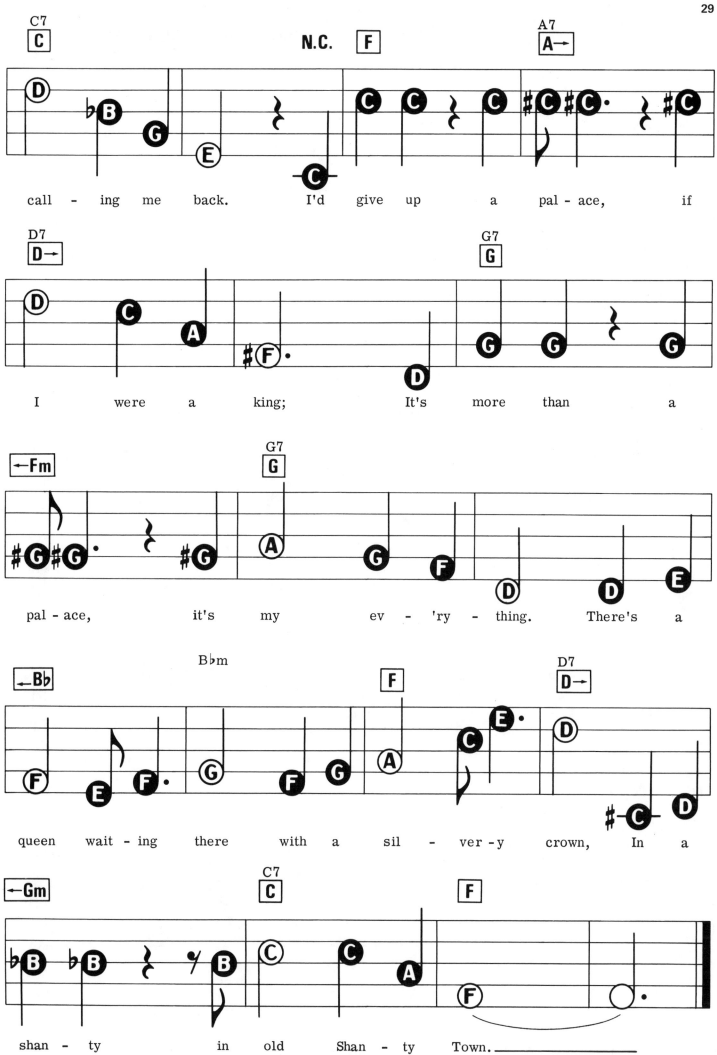

Let The Rest Of The World Go By

Words by J. Keirn Brennan
Music by Ernest R. Ball

Registration 5

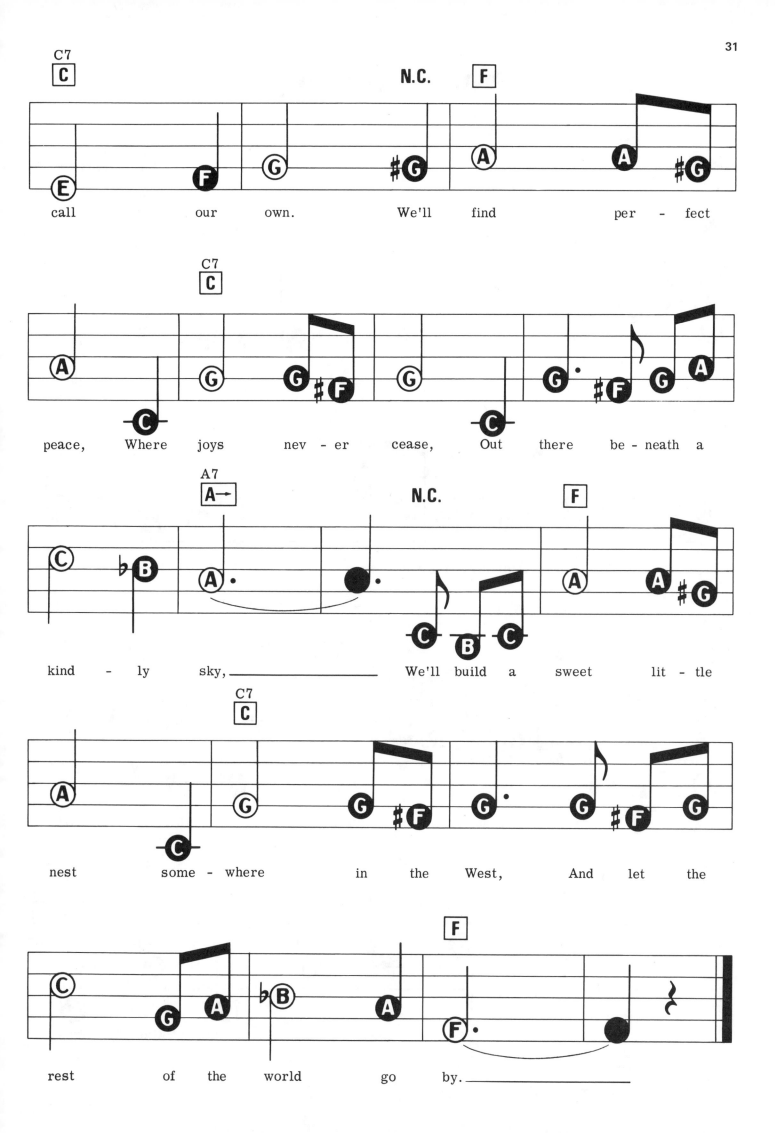

Moonlight Bay

Words by Edward Madden
Music by Percy Wenrich

Registration 2

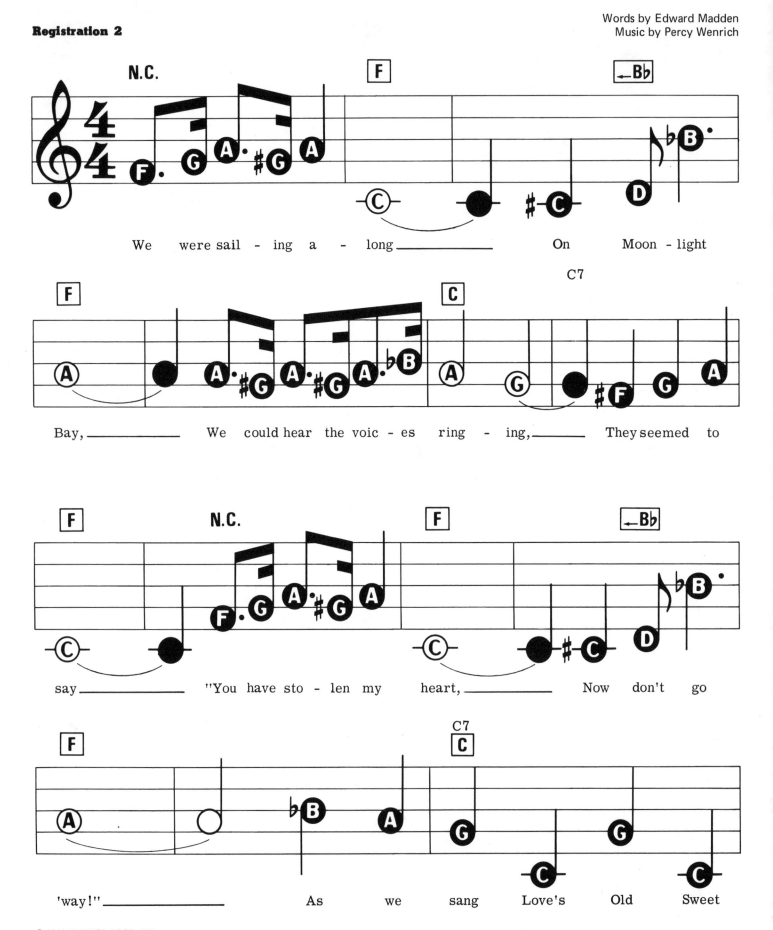

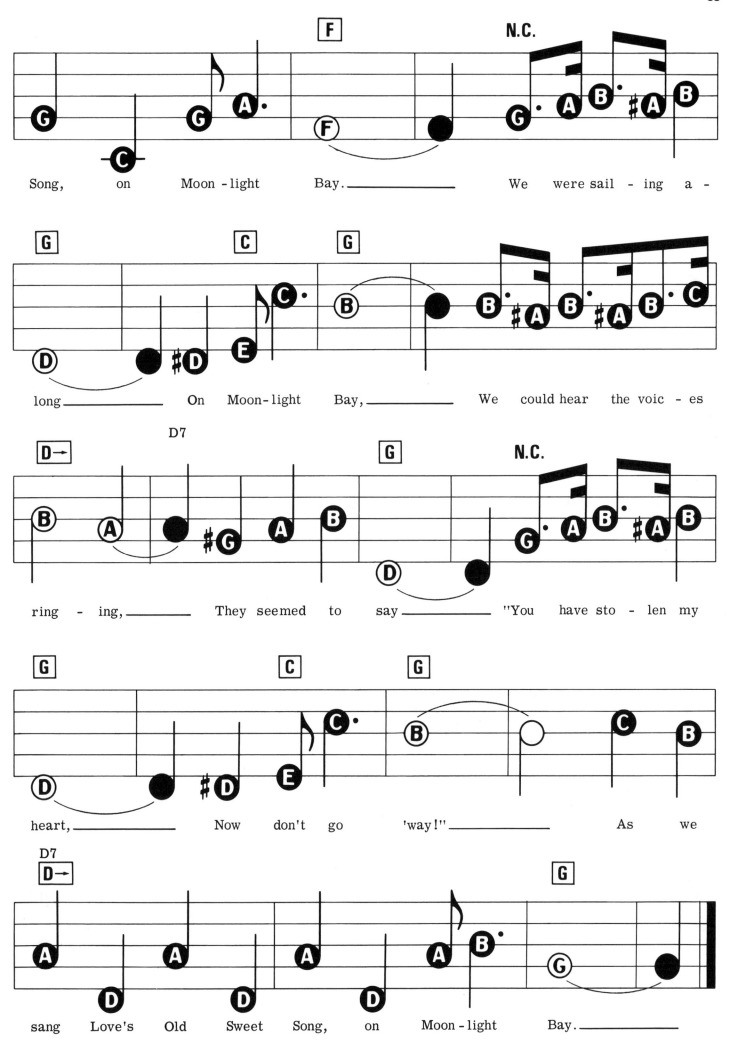

My Heart Stood Still

Words by Lorenz Hart
Music by Richard Rodgers

Registration 4

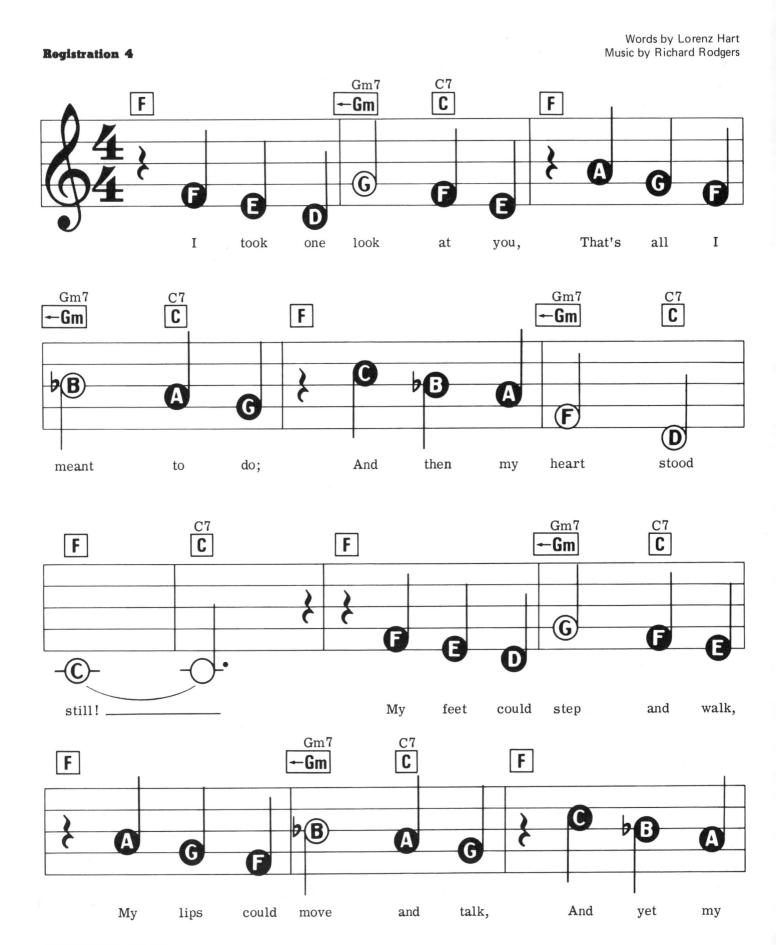

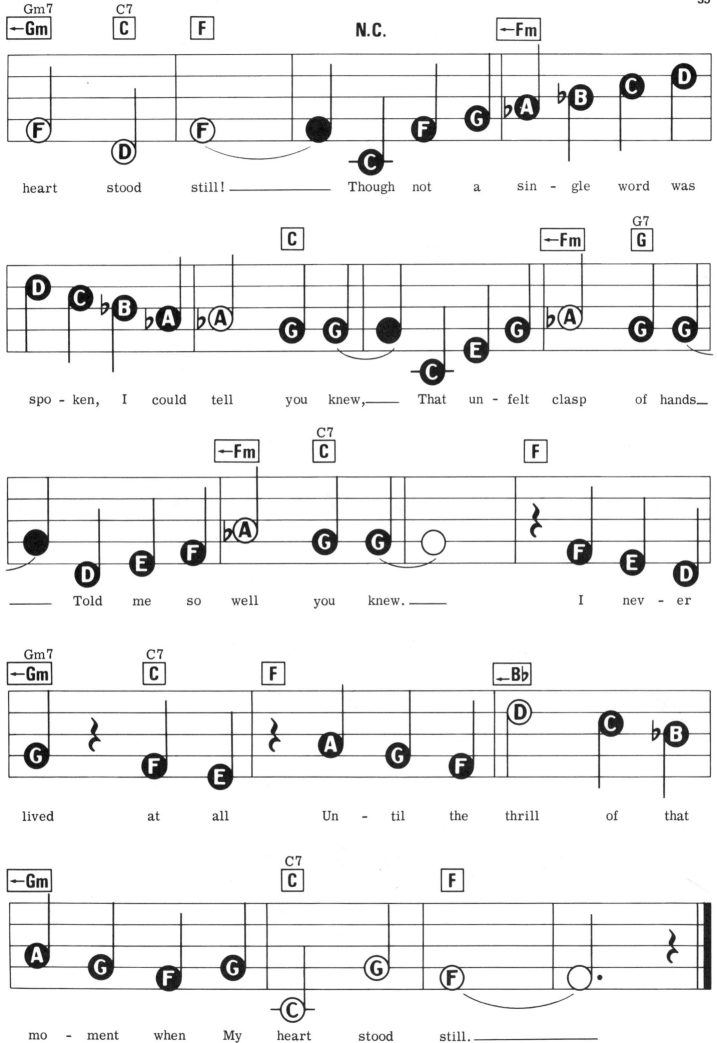

Oh! You Beautiful Doll

Words by A. Seymour Brown
Music by Nat D. Ayer

Registration 8

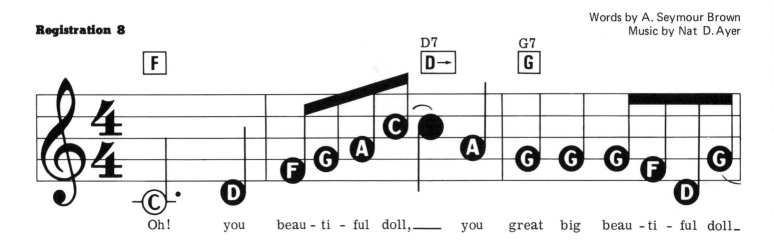

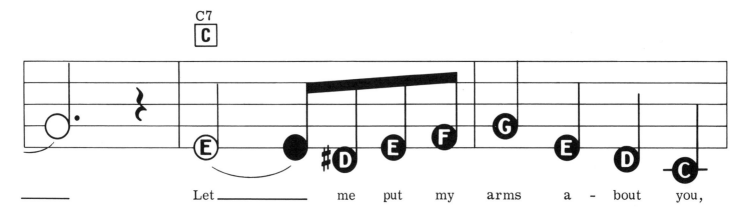

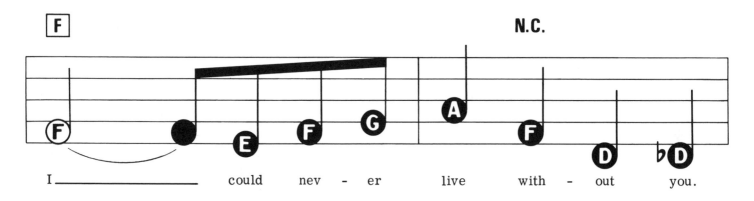

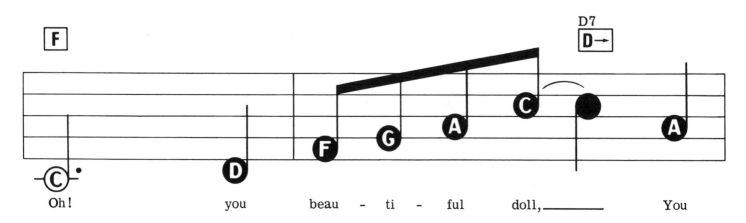

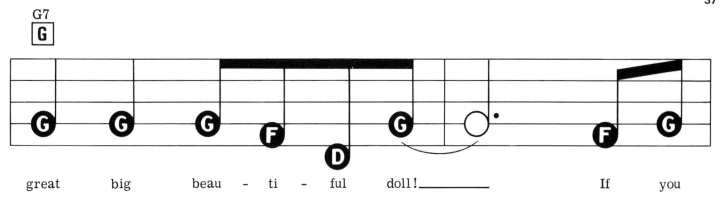

great big beau - ti - ful doll!_____ If you

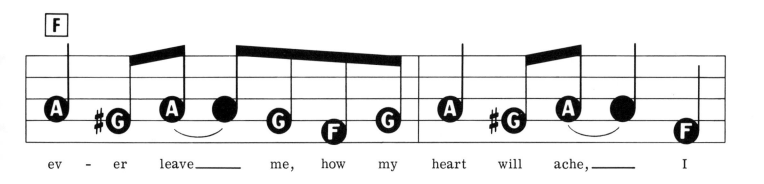

ev - er leave_____ me, how my heart will ache,_____ I

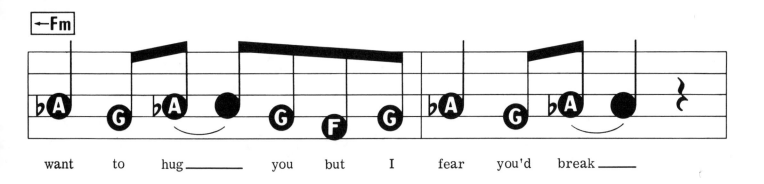

want to hug_____ you but I fear you'd break_____

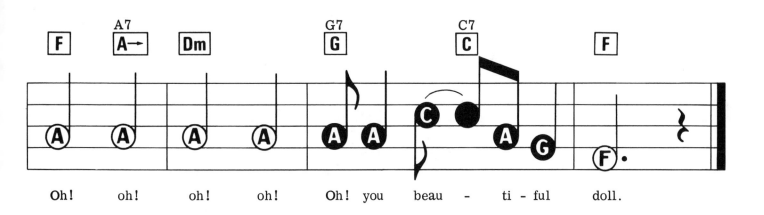

Oh! oh! oh! oh! Oh! you beau - ti - ful doll.

Pretty Baby

Registration 2

Words by Gus Kahn
Music by Egbert Van Alstyne and Tony Jackson

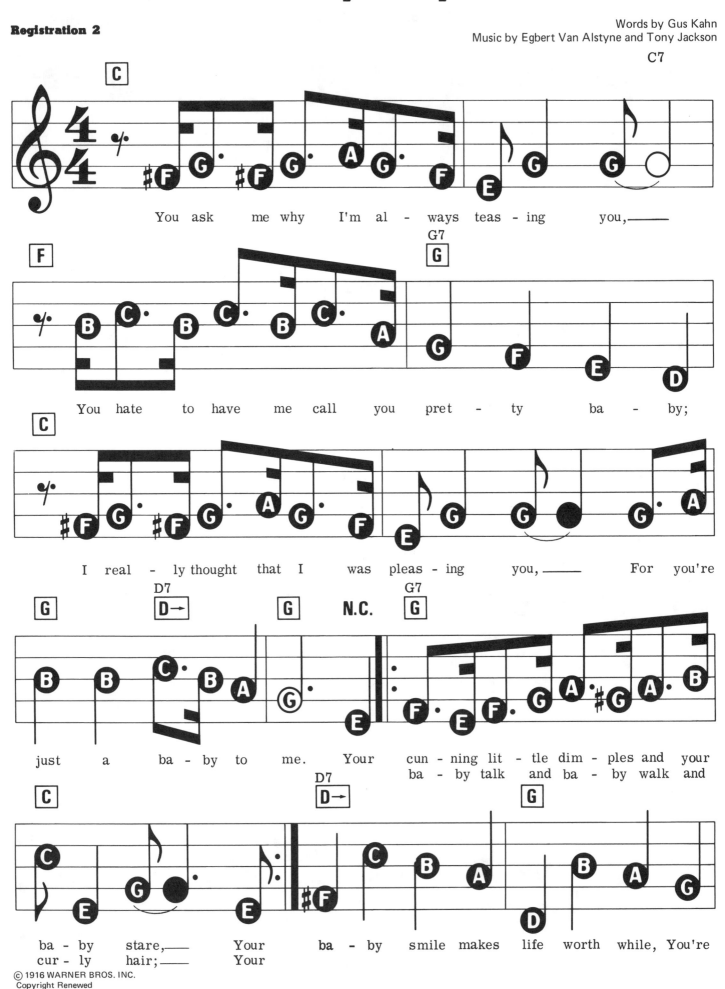

just as sweet as you can be. Ev-'ry-bod-y loves a ba-by that's why
like to be your sis-ter, broth-er,

I'm in love with you, pret-ty ba-by, pret-ty ba-by; And I'd
dad and moth-er too, pret-ty ba-by, pret-ty

ba - by, Won't you come and let me rock you in my cra-dle of love,— And we'll

cud - dle all the time. Oh! I want a lov-in' ba-by and it

might as well be you, pret-ty ba-by of mine.

Put On Your Old Grey Bonnet

Words by Stanley Murphy
Music by Percy Wenrich

Registration 3

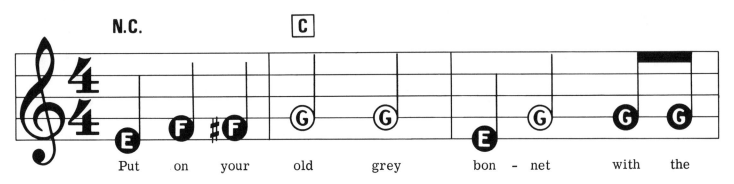

Put on your old grey bon - net with the

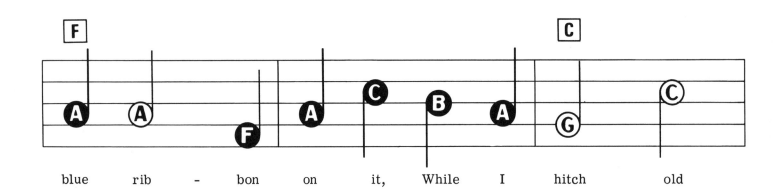

blue rib - bon on it, While I hitch old

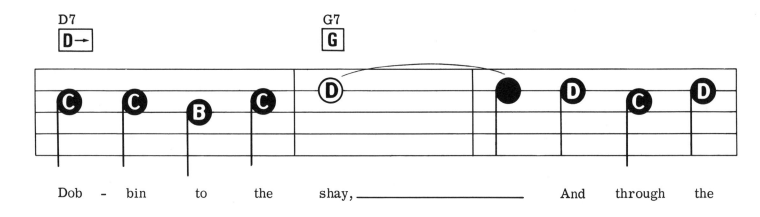

Dob - bin to the shay, _____ And through the

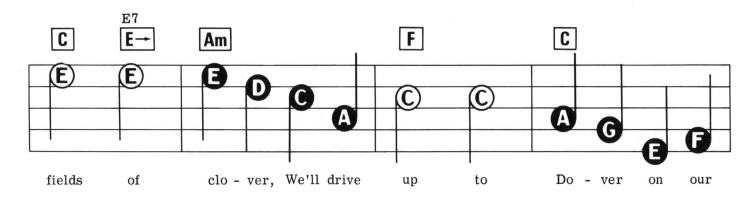

fields of clo - ver, We'll drive up to Do - ver on our

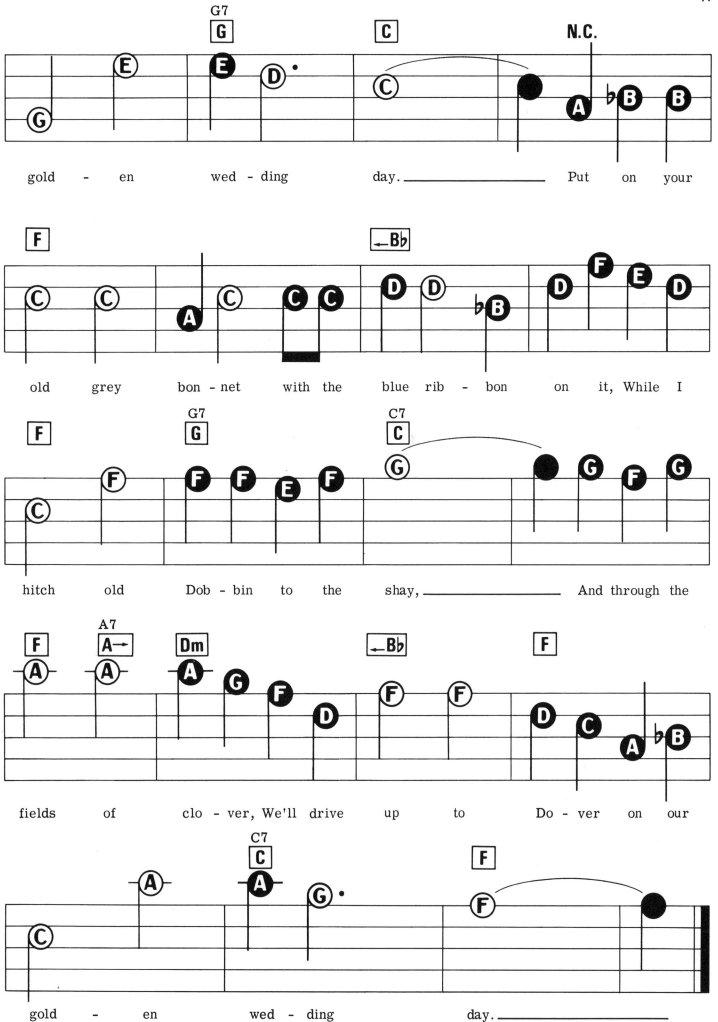

Smiles

Words by J. Will Callahan
Music by Lee S. Roberts

Registration 5

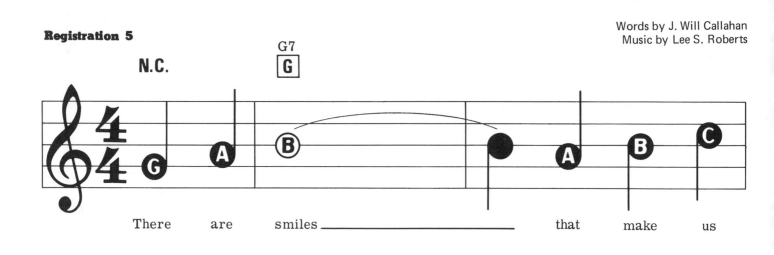

There are smiles _____ that make us

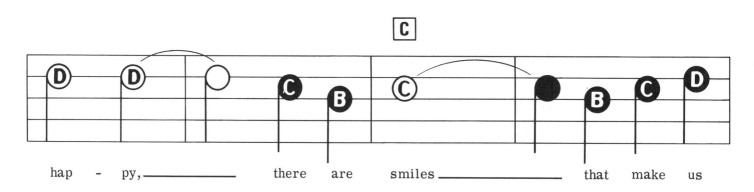

hap - py, _____ there are smiles _____ that make us

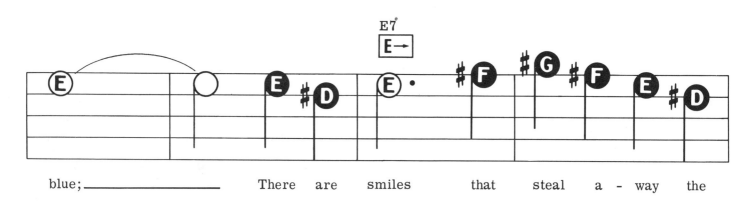

blue; _____ There are smiles that steal a - way the

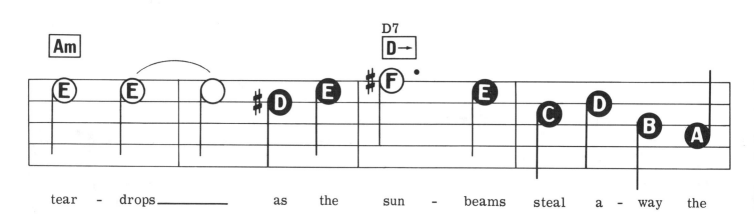

tear - drops _____ as the sun - beams steal a - way the

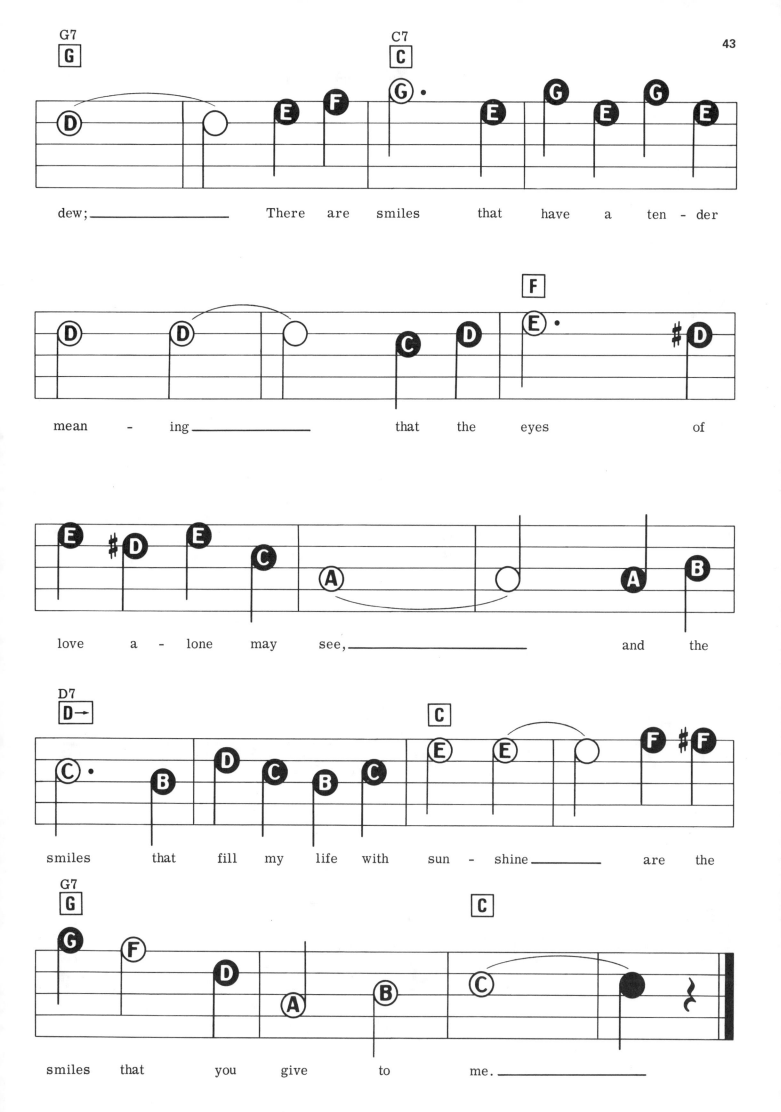

Till We Meet Again

Words by Raymond B. Egan
Music by Richard A. Whiting

Registration 4

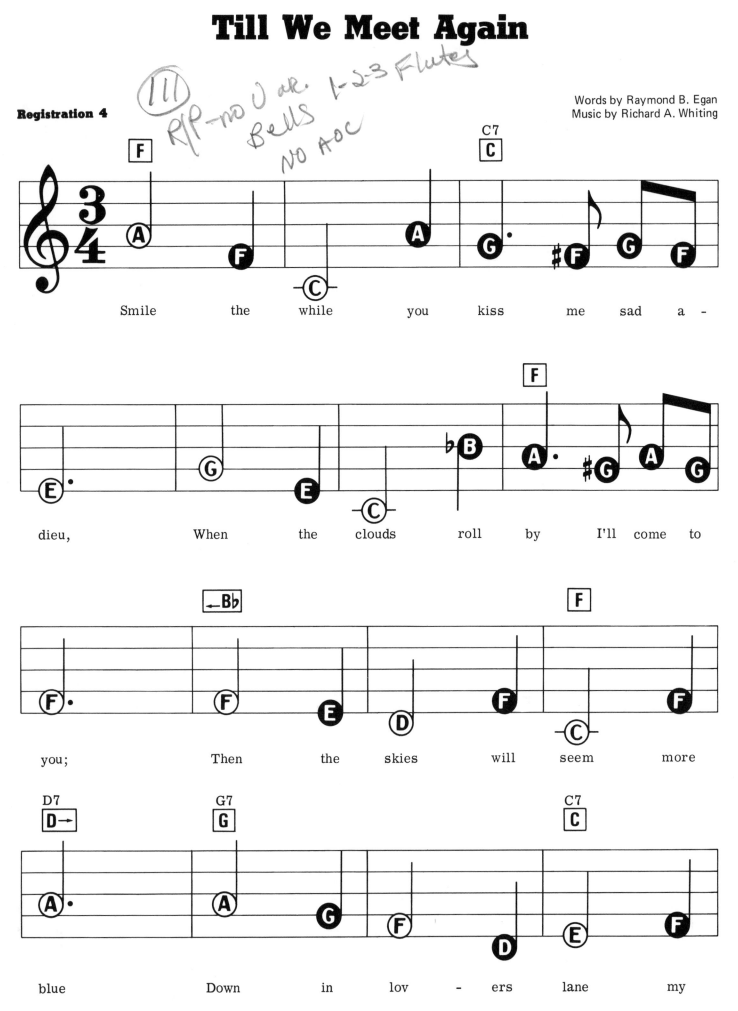

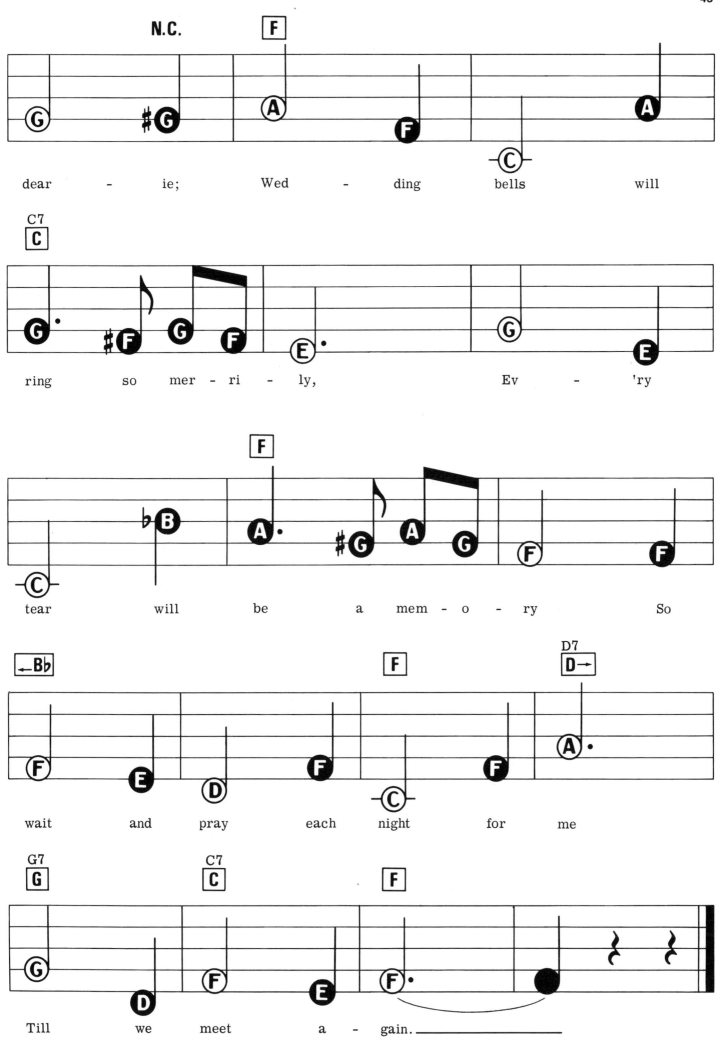

Guitar Chord Chart

To use the E-Z Play TODAY Guitar Chord chart, simply find the **letter name** of the chord at the top of the chart, and the **kind of chord** (Major, Minor, etc.) in the column at the left. Read down and across to find the correct chord. Suggested fingering has been indicated, but feel free to use alternate fingering.

	F♯	G	A♭	A	B♭	B
MAJOR						
MINOR (m)						
7TH (7)						
MINOR 7TH (m7)						

Chord Speller Chart
of Standard Chord Positions

For those who play standard chord positions, all chords used in the E-Z Play TODAY music arrangements are shown here in their most commonly used chord positions. Suggested fingering is also indicated but feel free to use alternate fingering.

CHORD FAMILY Abbrev.	MAJOR	MINOR (m)	7TH (7)	MINOR 7TH (m7)
C	5 2 1 G-C-E	5 2 1 G-C-E♭	5 3 2 1 G-B♭-C-E	5 3 2 1 G-B♭-C-E♭
D♭	5 2 1 A♭-D♭-F	5 2 1 A♭-D♭-E	5 3 2 1 A♭-B-D♭-F	5 3 2 1 A♭-B-D♭-E
D	5 3 1 F♯-A-D	5 2 1 A-D-F	5 3 2 1 F♯-A-C-D	5 3 2 1 A-C-D-F
E♭	5 3 1 G-B♭-E♭	5 3 1 G♭-B♭-E♭	5 3 2 1 G-B♭-D♭-E♭	5 3 2 1 G♭-B♭-D♭-E♭
E	5 3 1 G♯-B-E	5 3 1 G-B-E	5 3 2 1 G♯-B-D-E	5 3 2 1 G-B-D-E
F	4 2 1 A-C-F	4 2 1 A♭-C-F	5 3 2 1 A-C-E♭-F	5 3 2 1 A♭-C-E♭-F
F♯	4 2 1 F♯-A♯-C♯	4 2 1 F♯-A-C♯	5 3 2 1 F♯-A♯-C♯-E	5 3 2 1 F♯-A-C♯-E
G	5 3 1 G-B-D	5 3 1 G-B♭-D	5 3 2 1 G-B-D-F	5 3 2 1 G-B♭-D-F
A♭	4 2 1 A♭-C-E♭	4 2 1 A♭-B-E♭	5 3 2 1 A♭-C-E♭-G♭	5 3 2 1 A♭-B-E♭-G♭
A	4 2 1 A-C♯-E	4 2 1 A-C-E	5 4 2 1 G-A-C♯-E	5 4 2 1 G-A-C-E
B♭	4 2 1 B♭-D-F	4 2 1 B♭-D♭-F	5 4 2 1 A♭-B♭-D-F	5 4 2 1 A♭-B♭-D♭-F
B	5 2 1 F♯-B-D♯	5 2 1 F♯-B-D	5 3 2 1 F♯-A-B-D♯	5 3 2 1 F♯-A-B-D